Lion's Roar

Written by Jeanne Willis
Illustrated by Derek Collin

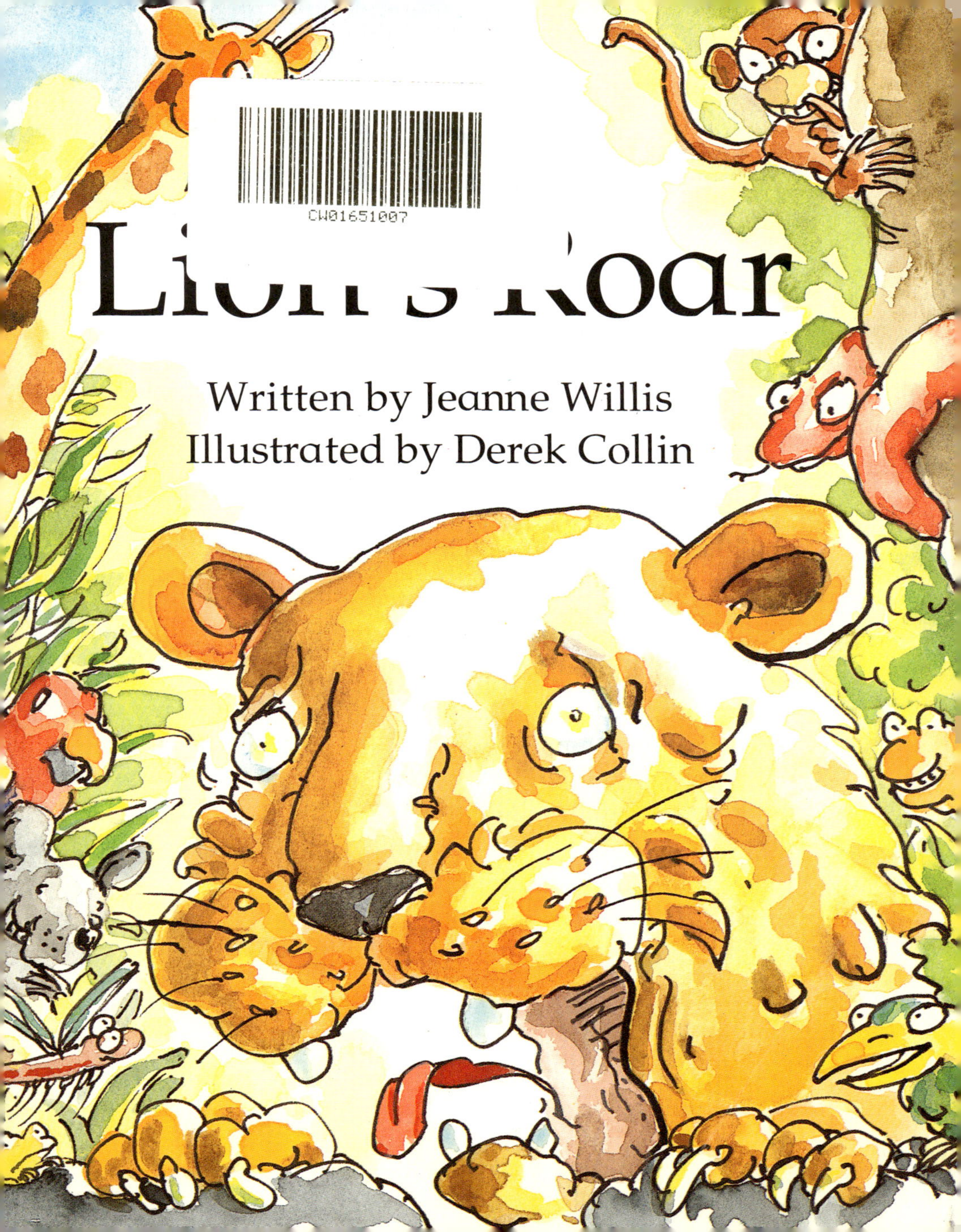

There was a little lion
who did not have a roar.
He tried and tried and tried and tried
until his throat was sore.

The little lion felt so sad.
He felt so sad and small.
What is a lion without a roar?
He's not a lion at all.

He went to see a doctor.
The doctor was a snake.

The little lion opened wide,
and ate her by mistake.

He went to see a dentist.
The dentist was a mouse.
When he saw the lion's teeth,

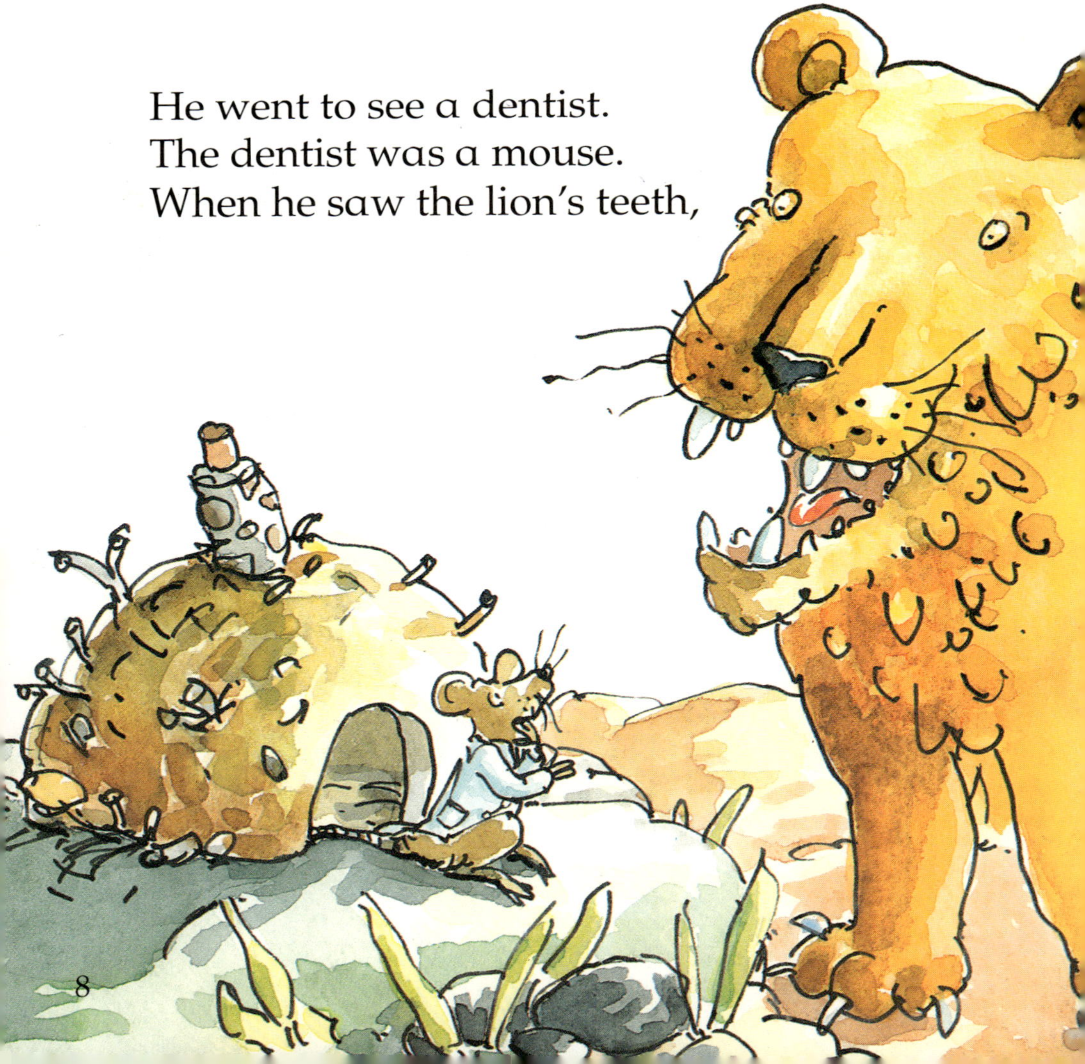

he hid inside his house.

The little lion felt so sad.
He felt so sad and small.
What is a lion without a roar?
He's not a lion at all.

He went to see a wise man.
The wise man was an ox.
When he saw the lion's claws,
he jumped behind some rocks.

The little lion ran away.
He ran away to hide.

The little lion tried to roar.
He could not and he cried.

The little lion felt so sad.
He felt so sad and small.
What is a lion without a roar?
He's not a lion at all.

Then a jungle sparrow
hopped on to his head.
'I can show you how to roar.
Follow me,' she said.

The little lion followed her,
up a hill and down.

Round and round a mountain,
in and out of town.

The little lion followed her
to a sandy bay.
The jungle sparrow said, 'Goodbye.'
Then she hopped away.

The little lion felt so sad.
He felt so sad and small.
What is a lion without a roar?
He's not a lion at all.

'Listen to me, young lion,'
roared a giant wave.
It sounded like a hundred lions,
big and bold and brave.

The little lion listened
to the roaring of the sea.
'This is how to roar,' it said,
'Lion, roar like me.'

The little lion shut his eyes,
and roared with all his might.
He roared and roared and roared and roared.

At last, his roar was right.